I0474994

CONTACT CENTER AGENT 101:

An introduction to your multi-channel call center career

By Steve Stapp

Contact Center Agent 101

CONTACT CENTER AGENT 101:

An introduction to your multi-channel call center career

Copyright © 2009 Steve Stapp

First Edition

Contact Center Agent 101

Table of Contents

Contact Center Agent 101

Contact Center Agent 101

Contact Center Agent 101

viii

Contact Center Agent 101

Forward

This book is dedicated to the front line agents in a contact center. I was inspired to write this book by my mother Mary, who has spent nearly two decades working as a front line contact center agent. Mary's enthusiasm for excellent customer service and the enjoyment of her work is contagious to those around her. Mary truly enjoys people and has made a fulfilling career in this rapidly growing industry.

Mary and I have had many discussions over the years as to why things are done the way they are in the contact center from an operational perspective. From these and many other discussions, a realization came to mind that there was often a missing link regarding the communication from leadership to agents of why things are done the way they are in a contact center. In addition, there is so much that makes up a contact center that the front line agents miss out on because they are never exposed to the inner workings and opportunities. The spirit of these conversations are now being shared with you in hopes your contact center experience will be one you will enjoy for many years, just like Mary.

The purpose of this book is to give you an introduction to your wonderful career ahead of you in a contact center. You will learn many things from the types of contact centers that exist, to basic terms and what life is like working in a contact center. You will also gain a basic understanding of contact center technologies and career opportunities that are available to you. Most importantly, you will learn why many of the things are done the way they are in a contact center. This understanding can enrich your initial experience and lead you to a wonderful new career.

Wishing you much success,

Steve Stapp

Part One:
An Introduction to Your
Contact Center Career

- WELCOME!
- WHY DO CONTACT CENTERS EXIST?
- DO I HAVE WHAT IT TAKES?
- WHAT WILL I BE DOING?
- WORKING ENVIRONMENT
- RESEARCH COMPANY BEFORE YOU START YOUR JOB
- WHAT TYPES OF CONTACT CENTERS EXIST?

Contact Center Agent 101

Welcome!

Congratulations as you embark in your new career in the rapidly growing contact center industry. In the event you are simply researching the industry in your desire to learn more about it, a warm welcome is extended to you. In either case, what you are about to review are the inner workings of a contact center from a "production employee" perspective. In this case we are referring to a production employee as a person who completes the end work either directly with a consumer or from a support role.

Much has been written about contact center technology, management, and strategic planning. This book however is for you, the person who ultimately makes a contact center tick. You will learn about various terms used in the industry as well as why things are done the way they are. This book is purposely written in simplistic terms so that someone without contact center experience can understand. Without this understanding of why things are done the way they are, some inner workings of a contact center could seem very frustrating.

For those of you already in the industry and possibly leading the production employees, use this guide as a how to explain the inner workings of a contact center to people. People like to understand the why behind things and will work very hard if they understand the big picture. If people are simply told to do something because that is the way it is, you might as well just place another job posting now because loyalty will be a thing of the past and you will soon be replacing your staff.

Whether this is your first experience in a contact center or if you are a seasoned veteran, this book should give you insight as to the dynamics that make a contact center tick. And tick they do, some like a broken down truck and others like a well-oiled machine.

Throughout this book, the term agent will be used to refer to the person working on the phones. Companies have many terms for this position; some are referred to as agents, specialists, consultants, customer service representatives, or team-members. Whatever the name given to this position, understand this is truly the most important position in the contact center industry. Why is that you say? Well imagine for a moment if you will, a nice building, an expensive phone system, great advertising, customers calling in to purchase or inquire about the company's wonderful products, and there are not any agents in the building! This wouldn't make very good customer service now, would it? You, the production employee are critical to the overall success of the organization. That being said, you also have an obligation to provide value back to the organization as well. It is your responsibility to provide value back to your company in the terms of sales and/or service so they can succeed and continue to provide employment to you.

Why Do Contact Centers Exist?

Let us begin with taking a look at the reason a contact center exists and ultimately the reason the position of agent exists in the first place. Realize contact centers are very expensive to operate no matter what the reason for their existence. The bottom line reason they exist is to add value to the organization whether to provide customer service to existing or prospective customers or to generate sales that lead to revenue for the company. It is important to keep this value proposition in mind so we don't become complacent with coming to work and going through the motions. Often times the contact center is the very first experience a prospective customer has with an organization and regardless of the size of the company, you as an agent, may very well be the very first impression someone has of your company. We have all heard before you never get a second chance to make a good first impression. Think about our interaction with your customer and/or prospect for a moment. You may be the individual who provides the first impression a prospective customer has of a small or a multi-billion dollar corporation. This potential or existing customer may be getting ready to place a very small order or an order worth millions of dollars in revenues. Quite a responsibility you have now, isn't it?

How much value will *you* add to the revenue tree?

Do I Have What it Takes?

What personal attributes might a person who fits into a contact center have? First, you should enjoy people; you will talk to hundreds and thousands of people over your career and if people are something like nails on a chalkboard to you then you may consider another career such as computer programming, warehouse work, construction or manufacturing or any other type of career where your customer interactions are limited. Now if you not only enjoy people, but you enjoy helping people, then a contact center career may very well be for you. In the true spirit of a contact center you are there for the benefit of the consumer. The consumer will then derive their benefit by your service to them in helping them solve whatever problem or desire they have.

Enjoying structure is another attribute that could lead to your success in the contact center industry. Structure in the form of when to work, scripted language or guidelines that must be followed, even certain key strokes may be recommended from an efficiency standpoint. One point to keep in mind is even though many contact centers are quite structured, adaptability and willingness to change are two other attributes that will help you maintain your sanity in this rapidly changing world we live in. As new marketing programs or computer systems are rolled out, the way that you perform your job may require you to adapt to these changes.

Some environments such as sales would require you have the attribute of being goal driven. Being goal driven may not only help you earn excellent reviews but can also have an impact on your pocketbook depending on the compensation package of your company. Goals other than just sales goals may also exist such as quality or schedule adherence (explained in detail later) goals may also be measured. Goals are put in place as both motivation and to ensure the company remains strong and profitable, which will in turn strengthen your job security.

It has been said that attitude is everything. Attitude may not be the only factor in consideration for your career and in your life but having the right attitude can certainly give you the edge in everything you do. A positive attitude will have you arriving to work on time. A positive attitude will have you react positively to change. A positive attitude will help to give you better ratings on job reviews. A positive attitude will help set you apart from others should you seek opportunities of advancement. Finally, a positive attitude will make people want to be around you and isn't it more fun to have these types of people around you.

If a positive attitude makes such a difference, how does a person get a positive attitude in the first place? Many factors lead to a positive attitude. First, a proper diet and regular exercise will help fuel your body to feel the best it possibly can. Take care of your body and mind and it will help take care of you. Second, surround yourself with positive people and distance yourself from gossipers and negative people. Negative people love to share their misery. Make certain you take no part in their pity parties. Read positive books and listen to motivation or learning books/seminars on tape. Finally, get your finances in order. Nothing creates stress and a poor attitude faster than financial troubles. Dave Ramsey (www.daveramsey.com), a nationally known financial advisor, and Money Magazine (www.money.com) are two excellent places to start taking charge of your financial future.

Personal responsibility is something many people think does not matter anymore. Personal responsibility does matter. Take responsibility for yourself, your actions, and where you are in your life. So many people go through life suffering from *yeahbut* disease. After something that does not go their way, such as a promotion or performance review, you will hear them say things like; *yeahbut* if I had a different supervisor; *yeahbut* if I only had better training; *yeahbut* so and so does such and such. Do you get the idea? You are the only person ultimately responsible for you, so take responsibility for yourself.

What Will I Be Doing?

Working in contact centers has a variety of tasks that are performed and are listed in detail throughout this book. It is important to understand though that the first and foremost task is to service the customers. This customer servicing may either be service or sales or a combination of the two. The primary function then is to speak to customers while you are on the phone.

You will be accessing some type of company database that will assist you with gathering information and recording transactions. Once you are done servicing one customer, you will then move on to servicing the next customer, and so on.

Let them hear you smile…

Working Environment

The environment of a contact center is indoor work. This is particularity attractive if you live in a climate that is very hot, rainy, snowy, cold, etc. Agents are positioned at some type of a workstation often referred to as a "pod" or a cubicle. The workstation will typically have a computer or terminal, and a telephone. The job requires much sitting with limited opportunity to wander around.

You should be the type of person that likes to have structure within your workday because contact centers tend to have regimented schedules. This means when you come in to work you will very likely be assigned to specific things to do at specific times including scheduled breaks and lunches. Some centers though may have variable start times from day to day. For instance, you may begin your shift at 7:00 am on a Monday morning and then Tuesday through Friday you may begin your shift at 8:00 am. Your breaks and lunches may have varied start times day to day as well. The reasoning behind these changes will be discussed in detail a bit later.

Buildings that contact centers are located in are very expensive and seating is at a premium. Some contact centers will have assigned seating where you will sit at the same place every day. Other centers will have what is referred to as open seating. Open seating is when you may sit at any open seat that is available at the time you come to work. Very large centers that use open seating sometimes will have a seating coordinator that works just like a host or hostess at a restaurant directing you where you will be sitting. This seating method is sometimes used to coordinate agents together in sections so supervisory support can be more readily available.

When call volumes are low or the centers are small sometimes traditional telephones are used by the agents. More commonly however, headsets are used so it is more comfortable for the agent. In addition, the sound quality for the customer tends to be crisper and has less background noise that is filtered through the mouthpiece. Headsets also reduce neck strain and are more ergonomically friendly.

Answering call after call in an inbound contact center, picking up the phone or manually answering the call by hitting a button can become quite repetitive and inefficient. To ease this repetitive process of manually answering the phone, an advanced telephone feature called zip tone may be used. Zip tone allows the agent to continue wearing their headset between calls and when a caller comes in, a type of tone or announcement of the caller is heard just prior to the call being passed along to the agent. The announcement may be the type of call or location of the call coming in. The announcement may even be the customer name in some environments. Zip tone also reduces the time required to answer calls making call answering more efficient at the center and ultimately providing faster customer service.

Just a note regarding the environment you work in; keep in mind you will be spending a great deal of time at work so out of respect for your co-workers and yourself, keep it clean! Now this does not mean (they are very busy but will often make time for you if you make an appointment) you have to go and get the mop but it does refer to common courtesies. If you spill something in the microwave, wipe it up; throw away paper towels and other disposables in the trash when finished with them; and remove your lunch from the refrigerators (if provided) nightly so they stay fresh and clean. These little things go a long way in keeping your work environment one that people enjoy going to on a daily basis.

Working in contact centers is no different than any other type of business with regards to one item, the rumor mill. Yes, we are talking about the ever-perpetuating water cooler conversations. In contact centers, the rumor mill can become quite infectious and the stories grand. This is due to the large number of people who may work in a single location and is also compounded when a multi-site environment exists. With multiple sites, rumors can start in one site and jump like wild fire to another location even in another state. The fact of the matter is, rumor mills can be quite detrimental to the morale and the well being of those working at the center. Much of the information being passed on is hearsay and simply not true. This misinformation can be damaging to the company and the employees involved. The best advice on this is to simply stop rumors in their track and not pass them along. You are encouraged to ask your supervisor or manager if you should ever desire to clear up any rumors.

Research Your Company

To position yourself for the best chance of success when you start with a new company, take some time and do some research about the company. If you have not yet started with a company and are getting ready to interview researching the company can help you answer interview questions intelligently as well as allow you to come up with some great questions.

If you have already secured your new job and are beginning training, learning about the company can still help you greatly. Training is a team effort and you must do your part to learn and the trainers will do their part to help you learn. You can learn about a company several different ways but two easily accessible methods are web sites and annual reports. Web sites and annual reports can give you volumes of information such as who the key executives are, what products and or services are sold, what the market position is, who the competition is, and what is the financial condition of the company? Once you have a foundation for the company you work for, learning will come easier to you when in the classroom because you will have an overall picture of where your contact center services fit in to the organization as a whole.

What Types of Contact Centers Exist?

Call center or contact center; what is the difference? While these terms are often used interchangeably, there is a fundamental difference between a call center and a contact center. A call center is an entity within an organization that handles either inbound calls from a customer or initiates outbound calls to customers. The nature of the work is all related to an agent being on the phone with a caller. A contact center on the other hand, has several different methods of communicating with customer and/or processing the work. For instance, an agent may communicate with a customer on the phone, through email or a chat room, or even with the use of faxed documents. When several of these methods are utilized in a contact center, the methods are referred to as multi-media communication.

Just as you cannot say the only flavor of ice cream is vanilla, contact centers have many different flavors as well. Some are even combined to make a contact center sundae! This is very important to understand; if for some reason you are not finding personal fulfillment in the contact center you are working in, you might simply be matched up with the wrong type for your distinct personality.

The two basic call types handled in contact centers are inbound and outbound calls. An inbound contact center is where customers of the company are calling the company for information, a product, or service. An outbound contact center is where the company initiates the call to the consumer. This consumer may be an existing customer or a potential customer the company is attempting to gain. This consumer may also be a person who owes money and the company is initiating a call to collect what is rightly theirs.

Let us first review one of the most fundamental contact center types; a Profit Center. This is just what it sounds like, the center is there to make a profit and just as important the accountants of the company look at it as such. What creates a profit for the company? Moving (selling) some type of product and/or service to the end consumer. Examples of products may be a catalogue order center or an infomercial product center, while services could include a large travel agency, or a computer assist line service.

The second major type of grouping for a contact center is that of a cost center. A cost center is typically an entity the accountants of the company have deemed cost the company money to operate rather than generate revenue. Do not despair. Just because a company has a contact center that is deemed a cost center, does not mean it is not important. These centers are often a necessary cost of doing business. Examples of cost center may be an airline flight information desk or a company's internal help desk. Typically in a cost center, it is not uncommon to see a constant focus on trimming costs and running more efficiently.

A Service Bureau, also known as an Outsourcer is an alternative or supplement a company may use to run their contact center operations. Companies may decide not to run their own contact center and contract out the work to a company that specializes in this type of work. The Service Bureau will supply the building and equipment. They will also handle all the recruiting, training, coaching, and act just as if they were the company the customer is calling. In fact, in most cases the consumer does not even know they are talking to an Outsource company but rather believe they are speaking with a representative from the original company they called. Service Bureaus can also assist with contact forecasting and scheduling if desired.

Companies will use Service Bureaus in two different ways. The first is they will not run any contact centers themselves but will turn all the functions over to the Service Bureau. The second manner in which they are used is to run their own contact centers for the bulk of the business and then utilize the services of the Service Bureau for seasonal or supplemental work on an as needed basis. This can be a cost effective way for a company to handle some and/or all of their business requirements.

Help Desk contact centers may either be procedural or in technology areas that can assist customers with computer hardware or computer application questions and/or repairs.

Two types of Help Desks exist; internal and external. An internal Help Desk would be one that services the employees of the company in which they work. An external Help Desk would be one that caters to end consumers. These may be set up as part of a service contract or by charging the user by the minute for services rendered.

Emergency Operation centers would operate for home security, police, fire, ambulance, etc. Typically, these centers must be very adequately staffed due to a fast response time expected and in some cases required by law.

Collections contact centers are simply that. They are set up to collect monies owed that are past due. A couple of types of collections contact centers exist. The first is referred to as first party collections. These contact centers are when the company owed the money is attempting to collect the money themselves. Third party collections are when a company separate from the company who is due the money is making the collection attempt. Typically, once a contact makes it to third party collections, the person who owes the money is much more delinquent on their account. Collections can be viewed as difficult or put in the proper perspective can be viewed as assisting a person to get their finances back in order and you are helping to make arrangements that will allow this to happen.

Charity contact centers solicit either money or donations for charitable organizations. In addition, some charitable organizations may sell tickets to some type of benefit where a portion of the proceeds go to the charity and the donors get something in return for their contributions.

A TDD, also known as Telecommunications Device for the Deaf are often set up within a contact center or as an entire center itself to communicate with people who are hearing impaired. The way these systems work is to have a person type into the teletype (TTY) device and the message goes to the device within the center. This message is then relayed out through a voice call or vice versa.

Inbound & Outbound Sales contact centers sell both products and services. Inbound sales centers have consumers that have chosen to contact because of some marketing campaign, catalogue, airline booking need, infomercial, etc. Outbound sales centers initiate the phone call to the prospective consumer in an effort to get them to purchase the product or service of the company. Quite often this may be insurance, carpet cleaning, credit cards, etc.

Fulfillment contact centers are those people who are responsible for taking care of the "back office work." This would also be an order-processing center. For instance, when someone orders a product from a catalogue, their order is then completed through fulfillment centers. These can also be centers when people have requested marketing or product information from a company. Rebate centers would also fall under this category.

As competition becomes fiercer in the marketplace, companies are reaching out to better service their customers. One method of better servicing customers is by setting up a multilingual contact center. This is normally set up with the native language as the primary contact type and then smaller groups of agents for the multilingual contact type.

PART TWO:
THE FOUNDATION OF YOUR CAREER

- **BUILDING A STRONG FOUNDATION FOR YOUR FUTURE**
- **HELP IS RIGHT AROUND THE CORNER**
- **CUSTOMER SERVICE TIPS TO MAKE YOUR LIFE EASIER**
- **TRUE CUSTOMER EXPERIENCE**
- **FIRE! A FUNNY STORY FROM THE AUTHOR**
- **STAYING OUT OF TROUBLE WHEN MAKING OUTBOUND CALLS**
- **A FEW BAD APPLES ARE PLAYING THE SYSTEM**
- **ARE WE DOING THINGS RIGHT?**
- **AFTER THE CALL ACTIVITY**

Building a Strong Foundation for Your Future

Knowledge about your company and products, as well as the requirements of your job will help make you a better employee. This knowledge will also allow you to enjoy your job much more than the anxiety of not knowing answers to the questions your customers ask of you. Training is where it all begins and is a two-way proposition. Your company has a responsibility to give you the company and product foundation and the resources to help you learn these. You as the employee, also have an obligation back to your company and the customers you service to apply yourself in training. This means paying attention in training class, participating by asking valid questions, and taking time outside of work to study. What? You mean study for work without getting paid? While a company cannot force you to do this, it is very reasonable a person will take some personal time to excel in their career field of choice. Imagine how many people go to college and pay thousands of dollars and study for hours for no employer at the end of the day. Apply yourself 100 percent and your chances of excelling rise dramatically.

Products

Product training will allow you to learn not only about the features of the product but also the benefit it has to the customer. For instance, a feature might be a non-stop flight but the benefit is it will get a customer to their destination much quicker and with less hassle than having to connect. Spend some time to learn about your product offerings, including the features and benefits and you will offer exceptional service that sounds conversational and non-scripted.

Competition

Knowing your competition can help you sell your product or service. Learn about the weakness of your competition and then incorporate your products strength in such way it plays to your company's product and/or service strengths. Whatever you do, never say anything bad about your competition. This is scarcity thinking and there is so much abundance among us we can all succeed quite well without having to degrade the competition. Stand on the merits of your products and or service and your ability to transfer this value to your customer.

Soft Skills

The little extras you do when speaking to a customer are known as soft skills. For example, being polite, using proper grammar, truly listening to a customer's needs, and saying thank you are all examples of soft skills. These will set you apart very quickly from an average agent to a superior agent.

Call Control

Learn how to take your customer through a guided tour of your sales or service process and you will be able to service more customers while at the same time offering them fantastic customer service. A key principle is, whoever asks the last question is said to be in control of the conversation. Control of a conversation is not a bad thing but rather leading a caller through your call is an important process. Understand the customer did not go to customer training and does not know what information is needed for you to assist them the best so you must ask these questions to get them from point A to point B. Call control also drives your handle time down, which saves your company money and increases customer service.

Know your systems

Would you be interested in having less stress at work? How about providing better customer service? Any chance you might like to increase your sales or reduce your call handling time? There is one easy tip that can help you achieve all these desires! Learn your company's database system they have set up for you. In its most basic form, it may be a 3 ring binder. The more complex systems may be referred to as Knowledge Base, Direct Reference System, SharePoint, or some proprietary name. This database system is the very toolbox in which you are able to go to and get the right tool to complete your job. Nothing is more frustrating than to not know the answer to a question asked and not know where to find the answer. Mastering the systems you use will help you tremendously in your job. These include any computer systems you use to make a sale or look up information on your product or service as well as the phone system you are on. By mastering these systems, you will better be able to focus your attention on your customer's needs rather than spending energy trying to figure out your systems. Also, in this information society we are living in today, it is almost impossible for someone to be expected to memorize all the details about your company and the products and/or services that are offered. Your available database can save you hours upon hours of frustration and make your life so much easier if you will simply commit yourself to learning the system.

WIIFM – The best service and sales technique ever

If there were one best sales tip that would increase your sales, it is WIIFM. In terms of your customer, all they really want to know from their perspective is, "What is in it for me?" Thinking and responding in terms of the other person will do more for your sales and customer service skills than any gimmicks you could possibly muster up. How does one do this? When you describe something to your customer whether it be a product or a service simply say to yourself as if you were the caller, "So what?" Then explain what is in it for them. This is also referred to as describing the feature and selling the benefit. An example would be you mention to your customer you are able to get them express shipping and then because you are thinking, "so what?" you immediately follow your factual statement with the benefit; "so you will be able to begin enjoying your new beautiful outfit for this weekend". The feature is the express shipping but what the customer really cares about is the personal benefit to them, which in this example is being able to have the product quickly so they can wear it and look wonderful at some special occasion.

Working with Challenging Customers – You want what?

We may not enjoy dealing with the fact not every caller we speak to will be as happy as the last person who won the lottery but nonetheless we must work with them respectfully. On the extreme end these callers are sometimes referred to as irate callers and the better you know how to deal with them the better off you will be. While your company may have an extensive training program to help you work through these challenging customers, these tips may offer a bit of assistance as well.

The first thing to keep in mind is these upset callers are not mad at you personally. What they are mad at is the situation they *perceive* themselves to be in. Notice, the term perceive is used. The customer may or may not really be in the perceived situation they see themselves in but perception is often reality.

Keep your tonality constant and avoid arguing back with the customer. Arguing with customers or raising your voice is like pouring gasoline on a lit candle that can soon become a disaster quickly. Next, work to disarm the irate caller. One effective technique is to listen and respond with empathy. Use phrases such as, "I understand how you feel" or "I can certainly see where you are coming from". This does not necessarily mean you agree with the customer but does let them know you are sensitive to their side of the story. After you have disarmed the customer and have truly listened to their side of the story, then you can begin working to fix their problem. Remember, saving a customer for a company is much less expensive than having sales and marketing go out and try to find a new customer. Also, a happy customer tends to tell few people about their experience while an unhappy customer may tell hundreds of people over time. The point is to look at irate customers as a challenge rather than a problem for you.

If you really want to score points with your supervisor or manager and help advance your career there is something you can do after dealing with an irate caller. Identify what caused the problem in the first place and come up with a solution you could recommend to the company to prevent this from reoccurring. You might even come up with a cost benefit analysis of your solution. Your new idea may lead to happier customers for years to come. The final positive note on coming up with solutions is you may also prevent having to deal with another irate customer in the future. Now this is something your coworkers will thank you for!

Help is Right Around the Corner

If you have a question or entry you need assistance with, you have several options for help available to you based on the environment you are working in. The first line of assistance may be instant messaging or chat rooms that are monitored to provide first level assistance. Another option may be to dial an assist queue, which is a group of highly skilled people available to answer these questions. Sometimes these calls go directly to front line operational supervisors. Finally, a common help option would be floorwalkers who are constantly walking through the center available for assistance at any time. The most important thing for you to know is help is available for you if you know where to look.

Customer Service Tips to Make Your Life Easier

Customers are not an interruption of our day but the very reason for our professional existence. Customers are everything, for without them we would not have any revenue and without revenue we would not have any jobs. As we get into the routine work of our jobs, this can be easy to forget. Remind yourself at every moment why the job you are performing is needed in the first place, to service customers. Treat each customer as you would want to be treated and you will go a long way to gain customer service points. Customer service can be anything from providing a product and/or service that someone is looking to acquire to a simple "please" and "thank you".

Listen – What was that?

Truly listen to what your caller is saying to you. Often times, we are so busy thinking about the next thing we are going to say, we miss the real request of the caller. Without knowing what the caller is wanting, then we are not equipped to provide them with their desired outcome.

If you have the latitude in your center, a good listening technique is to repeat back what a customer has told you. For instance, you might say to your customer, "So you are looking for a multimedia computer that is fast and will allow you to burn home movies to DVD. Is that correct?" This will let the caller know you truly heard what they were saying.

In a world of fast, low touch customer service, customers will embrace you greatly if they know you are listening to what they have to say. This will keep customers coming back for more of what your company has to offer.

All in a Name

Whenever possible, work the caller's name into your conversation. There is nothing-sweeter sounding then to hear our own name used when communicating with others. This tip will help you build rapport quickly with your customer/prospect.

True Customer Experience

Contact centers often live in a world of averages when reporting numbers. The average number of seconds it takes to answer a call, the average number of calls handled, the average quality score, etc. While averages are acceptable to use as a benchmark, they can also be deceiving. End of the day or monthly statistics may appear to be just fine when in reality the true customer experience (TCE) for each and every customer was not acceptable.

Let's take service level for example. Service level is defined as a certain number of contacts answered within a specified number of seconds. A common example of service level might be 80% of the contacts answered within 20 seconds or less. This metric allows for times of the day, mornings for example, being very busy and having callers on hold for several minutes, while the afternoon callers are answered right away. If you were the morning caller that had to wait for several minutes when you where calling right before going into work, would you care about the end of the day service level being acceptable because the afternoon customers got right through? Absolutely not! What about quality? If you receive lousy service from a company you have called, would you really care the average quality scores were acceptable? Absolutely not!

The point of TCE is each and every person that calls deserves the right to be serviced in such a manner that his or her single call makes a big difference. Remember the concept of true customer experience for each and every person you talk with and your customers will be absolutely thrilled with the consistent excellent service they are receiving.

Fire! A Funny Story From the Author

A funny story happened to me while working as an operations supervisor at a major airline. I was just getting ready to end a swing shift that ended at 11:00 pm and the supervisor phone rang. So the oncoming supervisor could get settled in for the night I went ahead and said I would handle this last escalated call. As it turns out this man was so upset about a flight he had booked and wanted it changed without paying the appropriate rate. At that time, customers had to pay the difference in fare, which was quite significant; this kept people from booking cheap off peak flights and then trying to change them for a more premium time. The flights were full and the options were limited which didn't help the situation at all. After about 90 minutes of going back and forth with the man and being called every name in the book as well as informing him there was nobody who would override this decision, he finally was persistent that I needed to call the CEO of the company at home. I was a bit humored because in the same breath he informed me that he knew the CEO personally, he also mispronounced his name. Letting the man know there was no reason I would call the CEO at 12:30 am, he became a bit smart with me and thinking he found the exception to the rule said, "Who would you call if the building were on fire? To which I replied, "Well frankly Sir, I would call the Fire Department because they are the only people I know who know how to properly put out a fire!" While I don't necessarily recommend you trying this, I was at my wits end and we ended the call shortly after this part of the conversation.

Staying Out of Trouble When Making Outbound Calls

If you happen to work in a contact center that makes outbound phone calls, you need to make sure you are aware of your companies "Do not call registry". These are customers that have filed with the government that they do not wish to be marketed to. This law went into effect on January 1, 2005 and protects consumers from unsolicited phone calls. Calling people who are on a do not call registry is against the law and you and/or your company can be fined if you fail to abide by this rule. Your company probably already has a very detailed database of this information. Additional information may be found online at www.ftc.gov/donotcall/ or www.donotcall.gov. Please note you should also check your local and state laws for restrictions as well. Your company will most likely take care of this for you so you can focus on servicing customers and/or prospects.

A Few Bad Apples are Playing the System

No, we are not talking about the latest video game when we refer to playing the system. Here we are referring to the few people who attempt to get around the systems in place to avoid work. Some agents will learn there are ways of putting yourself at the end of the call queue so there is more time between calls. An agent may hang up on a customer thinking they will lower their overall handle time. Other agents may leave their phone in a call taking state and get up and go on a smoke break. Agents have even been known to pretend their headset is not working and say, "Hello? Hello? Are you there? Can you hear me?" When in reality their phone is working just fine. All these examples are simply techniques of avoiding work. At most companies these are grounds for immediate discipline up to and including termination. Understand that while a person may get away with these behaviors for a short period of time, there is nothing that can be done that is news to the leadership team. With the technology available these days, each one of these activities is easily caught. The sad part is the work being avoided does not go away; it simply goes to one of an agent's coworkers. If you should happen to be one of the very few people who are considering these behaviors, your career choice should be reviewed first so you do not even think about these actions in the first place. Be fair to your coworkers and be fair to yourself.

Are We Doing Things Right?

What do you mean people are going to listen to my calls? What about my privacy? Call monitoring is a normal part of contact center operations. Call monitoring is not used for spying on people but rather for quality control and training purposes. Call monitoring allows a supervisor or a quality control team to listen to agents and basically "observe" the call that took place. The live call is then compared to what the company wants to take place and feedback is provided on the performance of the agent. The items being looked for during call monitoring are excellent customer service techniques, call control, proper documentation, offers to assist, or an attempt at additional sales.

When used properly, call monitoring and feedback is one of the most effective learning methods available. An agent may be told something a hundred times, but it is not until they hear it for themselves they catch the change that could make them better.

After the Call Activity

After the call activity or work, can take place in two forms. The first is which an agent completes once the conversation with the caller is over. An example might be after taking some type of escalated or complaint call, a specific form might have to be completed and turned into a supervisor.

The second type of after call activity may be what is referred to as fulfillment work. Fulfillment is the back office work that takes place to finish a customer's order. For instance, a customer may call and submit a claim for a prize they have won. The fulfillment department would verify the information, gather the prize, and prepare it for shipping.

Part Three: Ensuring the Right People are in the Right Place at the Right Time Working on the Right Activity

- **THE BEAN COUNTERS - KEY PERFORMANCE INDICATORS OR KPI'S**
- **BEING AT THE RIGHT PLACE AT THE RIGHT TIME**
- **BEING THERE WHEN YOUR CUSTOMER NEEDS YOU**
- **BUT I WAS ONLY GONE FOR A MINUTE!**
- **WHERE DO I RANK?**
- **I WANT TO GO ON VACATION**
- **GIVE ME A BREAK!**
- **HOW DO I GET MY SCHEDULE?**
- **HOW MANY AGENTS DO WE NEED?**
- **WHAT IS ALL THAT TECHNICAL STUFF?**

The Bean Counters - Key Performance Indicators or KPI's

Say what; KPI's? Sounds like someone who was chosen to wash dishes at the mess hall. KPI's or, Key Performance Indicators are like watching a heart monitor in the operating room. These are the vital statistics that let the decision makers of the contact center know if they are doing a quality job from a customer service and an efficiency perspective. KPI's are often reviewed daily, weekly, monthly, and yearly. Let us take a moment and review some of the more common key performance indicators you may hear about.

Key performance indicators are detailed into two groups; those you personally have control over and secondly those out of your direct control but just as important to the leadership of your center.

The first KPI you have some control over is Average Handle Time (AHT). Average handle time is simply that time an agent is on a call including talk time, work time, and hold time (more on these in a moment) AHT is most commonly reported in seconds. The first component of AHT is Average Talk Time (ATT). Average Talk Time is simply the time an agent is on the phone talking or listening to a customer. The second component of AHT is Average Work Time (AWT). This may also be referred to as after call work time or wrap up, as in wrapping up the call. In any case, AWT is the time following a call an agent has placed themselves in an idle state so they may complete some type of work related to the call they were on. Most commonly, this is putting notations into the record or filling out some type of paperwork that could be completed without keeping the customer on the phone.

The final component of AHT is hold time. When an agent is talking to a customer and for some reason, places the caller on hold (maybe to make an outbound call or get some type of answer), this time is counted as average hold time.

First of all, why would anyone care how many seconds you are on a call and what can you do to make sure you are keeping your handle time down? When a retail store for example, staffs their departments, they are staffing based on a ratio of sales or customers to the retail staff. In a contact center, one of the metrics used is the length of customer transaction, or AHT, as we now know. The longer the AHT (even by a second or two), the more agents are required to serve the same number of customers. In addition, facility, benefits, and telecommunication charges must also be paid out as well.

So now you know what AHT is, what can you do about keeping it within the goals set by your company? Well, talking faster you will be glad to know is not the answer. The real answer is call control. This means you are directing the flow of the call rather than letting the customer dance you around. Call control includes being knowledgeable about your product so you are not spending excessive time searching for answers. But there is much more to it than that. Your company will most likely instruct you to use an efficient and short greeting. Often times little superficial questions like asking someone how they are doing are eliminated. Finally, and the most critical thing to remember is the person who asks the last question is in control of the conversation. This should be detailed out in your training but let's look at an example so the concept is clear.

A customer calls in and an agent answers the phone:

Agent: "ABC Company, Bob".
Customer: "Hi Bob. How are you?"
Agent: "Fine, thank you. Are you calling today for service or product information?
Customer: "I am calling for service. Did you catch the ball game yesterday?"
Agent: "I did, and what a game. What is your customer identification number?"

And the conversation continues. Do you notice how the agent will politely answer the customer's side questions precisely and then redirect the customer to a question that leads them to the next step in the sales or service call? When done correctly, call control is a very pleasant experience because it leads the customer to exactly where they want to go.

What are the leaders looking at?

Now let us review some of the metrics that are very important to the leaders in a contact center.

"Service Level" is a common way in which contact center performance is reviewed. Service level is an indicator of how quickly customer calls are being answered. Service levels are defined by the percentage of calls answered within a specified number of seconds. For instance, a service level of 80/20 means the goal of the contact center is to answer 80% of all calls within 20 seconds or less. 75/15 would mean the goal is to answer 75% of calls offered within 15 seconds. Service levels are managed real time throughout the course of the day and reported daily, weekly, monthly, and oftentimes at an interval level such as every 15 or 30 minutes.

Numbers of calls abandoned (NCA) calls are those calls where the customer connected and for whatever reason made a decision to hang up before their call was answered. Abandoned calls are reviewed by the number of them as well as the percent of abandoned calls in relation the calls offered.

Average seconds to answer (ASA) are the number of seconds that an average customer will wait queue (in line) before their call is answered. Caller tolerance can vary by type of customer being served. A person may be willing to wait a while for computer software support, but when it comes to calling the Fire or Police department, or the phone operator, a customer does not wish to wait and wants their call answered right away.

Occupancy basically refers to the amount of time an agent is busy while they are signed into the phones. If calls were in queue and an agent were receiving one call after another, occupancy would be at 100% Occupancy goals are often targeted at around 80-85% so agents stay fairly busy but do have some breathing room between calls. An occupancy rate too high can burn agents out, while an occupancy rate too low is costly for the company. In reality what often happens is there are times of day that may run a very high occupancy rate, (Monday morning's for an airline for instance) and then other times of the day will run an occupancy rate lower than the goal.

Quality scores are determined by the contact center leadership and are reported using a quality monitor scorecard or review sheet. Your company will let you know what is important with regards to servicing their customers and how you will be accountable for these items. Then, periodically you will be monitored (or recorded) while on the phone with a customer and you will be reviewed for how well you are following your company's expectations. Monitors and resulting quality scores are great coaching tools that are very often tied to performance evaluations including raises. A recording of you is a great learning tool because there is no better way to coach yourself then to listen to yourself. You will identify things you do, say, and even tones you use that would never be discovered if you didn't hear yourself. Attention is given to quality to ensure all customers are receiving consistent service. Think back to how frustrating it was when you purchased a product from a company you had a positive experience with only to find out their quality was hit and miss. For instance when ordering food, you are expecting hot fries and in reality they have been sitting out and are cold. When you get home ready to enjoy your meal, great frustration would be an understatement about the company you just bought them from.

A word about averages, you will have some calls that tend to be very short and you will have some calls that tend to be quite long. As long as you focus on those things your company trained you on regarding how to handle a call, and you focus on call control, your personal average numbers should work out just fine. What this really means is you shouldn't have to worry too much about getting stuck on an occasional long call you may think is driving your personal statistics up and out of the goal range.

Being Where You Are Supposed to be at the Right Time

Schedule Adherence is another key metric you as an agent have great control over. Agent schedule adherence is adhering to one's schedule of activities throughout the course of the day. Times measured for adherence are typically the start and end of a work shift, the start and end of a break or lunch, and other activities such as meetings and or any back office or ticket work you may have been assigned to do.

Adherence is pretty darn straightforward. If you are scheduled to be working on a specific activity at a specific time, then work on that activity when scheduled and you will score big points with your leadership team. The only real time that can possibly create a schedule that has to be manually adjusted is if an agent is stuck on a call working with a customer when another activity comes up. You would obviously not hang up on the customer and would report this to your supervisor or workforce team for a possible adjustment.

Looking at schedule adherence from another angle, it is more like managing availability rather than adherence. So what does this mean? Schedules are originally created by aligning the shifts and all the associated activities against the time that the customers are forecasted to be calling in. This process includes spacing out activities so there are still plenty of agents on the phone available to take a customer's call. The more your fellow coworkers adhere to their schedule, the more staff will be there to assist you when calls are coming in. If all things are done just right, this will have you working with some available time in between calls. The inverse is also true. If you happen to not take your break or lunch at the time it was scheduled, then your coworkers may have to work that much harder to stay on top of the call volumes because you are not there to help them service the customer.

Agent adherence to schedule is one of those things that may seem like management is simply getting after people. In reality is very important to excellent customer service. Why can't agent's get up and take breaks whenever they want to? Let's look at why that is. Take for instance a person working a gate an airline. This gate agent is standing there with a line of people in front of them and out of the blue the agent decides to just leave their position and take an unscheduled break, so they walk away from their line of people. Most people would never think of doing that. After all, customers are waiting and you can see them right there. Well, a contact center is really no different at all. The same line of people that were standing at the airport were in line with the reservation department to book their flight. Imagine these same people in line to have their call answered and agents decide to get up and walk away from them at their own free will. It happens, because the customers are not seen but they are truly there waiting. Now, if only one agent did this, it might be no big deal but what if you start to multiply this over many agents; now you have some upset customers because they believe the contact center was not staffed properly. The moral of the story is to work the shift and activities you are assigned throughout the day.

Being There When Your Customer Needs You

Scheduling begins with contact forecasting. Contact forecasting is the art and science of predicting when people will contact your company either through a phone call, email, chat, etc., for services. The contact forecast is important because it identifies when agents are required to be staffed in the center. This includes both long and short term forecasts as well as how many contacts are predicted to arrive every 15 or 30 minutes.

Contact forecasts can be quite complex and their accuracy is critical to effectively staffing an organization as well as keeping costs in line. While the purpose of discussing call forecasts is not to make you a forecasting expert, it will help you gain a clearer understanding of why your workforce or leadership team makes some of the decisions they make.

Forecasting is the projecting of future requirements for contacts (calls, emails, chat sessions, fax, etc), average handle time, and for people. The processing of forecasting begins with the long term forecast. The long term forecast is often projected for the next year, multi-year, and even sometimes up to five years for capacity planning purposes (how many seats and phone lines do you need for all the agents).

The first thing that goes into a contact forecast is reviewing historical data. These data are reviewed for accuracy before anything else is done or all future forecasts may be off. During this process, extraneous data are removed that could skew the numbers and lead to inaccurate schedules.

Once the data are deemed to be accurate, many variables will be studied and calculated. The first of which is seasonality. Seasonality is easily thought of in the airline industry. January is somewhat busy, February volumes drop as people have completed their end of year travels and the kids have started back to school. March, April, May, will have similar volumes and then comes summer time where volumes skyrocket. June, July, and August represent schools are out and families are traveling in droves. If you want to ride on busy airplanes, travel in the middle of the summer. Before these people traveled though, they were calling into the contact center. After summer, volumes drop as people are done with most of their summer travels. October picks up a bit but November and December get very busy with all the holiday travel. So if you were to look at airline volume for any given year, you will typically see standard patterns of calls that come in. Most businesses have some type of seasonality that will drive volumes for them as well so look to your specific industry for the seasonality patterns you will be faced with.

A growth rate is the applied that will show whether or not business is increasing (positive growth rate) or decreasing (negative growth rate), also called a declining growth rate. This can either be a specific number of contacts per month but is more often a percentage.

Company projects, advertising and marketing, completion, the economy, and many other drivers and events are reviewed and added into the calculation for forecasted contacts.

The calendar is reviewed to identify how many days in the month there are, how many business days in the month there are (weekends are usually not as busy as weekdays), and how many of each weekday there are in a month (a Monday is typically busier than a Wednesday for instance so you have to know how many you have.

These forecasted contacts are then applied to intervals throughout the day known as contact arrival patterns. Contact arrival patterns will reflect things like the fact many companies are busier on Monday morning than on Wednesday afternoon. The forecast will then apply predictions of future contacts accordingly.

The other thing to be aware of in a contact center is that contacts bunch up. Simply stated for any given half hour period, you may have agents sitting available waiting for a customer contact, and then all of a sudden many callers for instance pick up the phone and call all at once so now you have callers on hold. This is kind of like going to the grocery store and nobody is in line to check out until you are ready to check out. How in the world did all these people end up at the registers at the same time just when you got there? Customers in line at a grocery store bunch up and callers into a contact center bunch up as well. There are special formulas and calculators that will help forecast the impact of this but this topic is beyond the scope of this book.

Once the contact and AHT forecasts are calculated then the required numbers of agents are determined. This is calculated based on the number of hours an agent is available to work and then shrinkage factors are applied. Shrinkage factors? What the heck are shrinkage factors? Shrinkage factors are things like vacation time, sick days, training, meetings, etc.

But I Was Only Gone For a Minute!

The next time you are working in a contact center and you decide to leave your phone for "just a minute," stop for a moment and consider what the effect truly is. Let's say the average price of a product you were offering was $75.00 and assume an average call handle time of 5 minutes or 300 seconds to sell that product. Dividing the $75.00 by 300 seconds, the potential revenue is 25 cents per second, per agent. Over a one-minute time frame, the total potential generated revenue would be $15.00, however, this figure is based on the assumption every customer buys or a 100% sales effectiveness. Using a sales effectiveness of 25% meaning 1 out of every 4 calls results in a sale, the average potential lost revenue would be $3.75 per minute that an agent is away from their phones. Three-dollars and seventy-five cents may not seem like a big deal but if an agent spends one minute off the phones per day (50 weeks per year), it adds up to $937.50 in potential lost revenue per year. That is almost a thousand dollars per agent! This total equates to potential lost revenue of $93,750 per 100 agents your company employs. Please understand these numbers would have to be modified to your specific company but are simply given as an illustration to understand the power of a minute. So, the next time you think about leaving your phone for "only a minute," think about those thousand dollars that could be your next raise!

Where Do I Rank?

Seniority is often thought of as the longevity with a company. What often occurs is the longer someone is at a company the higher their seniority is said to be. The seniority position is often the hire date someone started with a company and some type of tiebreaker for those that began on the same day. Tiebreakers can be random number such as the last four digits of your social security number, or the month you were born. The tiebreaker may also be something that inspires someone to do well such as the test scores while in training.

Seniority can be used for determining bidding schedule position or vacation position. In addition, seniority may be used for same daytime off. Some companies may use a first come, first serve system, or may use a performance based criteria as an alternative.

I Want to Go on Vacation

Vacation time may be awarded on a first come, first serve, seniority, or performance based award system. Some companies will award the same number of vacation slots per day but more commonly the number of slots are varied based on customer demand. For instance, if Monday is a busy day in your center, then most likely there will be fewer vacation slots available for people to take off. Wednesdays may be slow days so many more agents are allowed to take this day off. Vacation slots based on business need also look at seasonality whereby the busy months of the year would allow fewer days off while slow months may have a great deal more days off offered to the agents.

The final element that is often looked at for allocating the proper amount of time off is the work type. For instance, if you have bilingual workgroups then a certain number of vacation slots would be offered to each workgroup. The business need of each workgroup may also be taken into consideration.

Give Me a Break!

Breaks and lunches are often scheduled for each shift an agent is working. The number of breaks an agent receives vary based on the number of hours that an agent is working and often vary by company. Some companies will have static breaks and lunches whereby an agent's breaks and lunches are scheduled at the same time every day and never vary. Other times though, breaks and lunches are optimized (spaced out based on need) to ensure adequate staffing to handle the customer contacts. Does it really make a difference to change the times that breaks and lunches are scheduled? It can actually make a significant difference in how quickly customer calls are answered. In a nutshell, what happens when breaks and lunches are optimized is that all the people who are out on vacation, in training or meetings, etc., will be taken into account as well as any meetings or trainings that are scheduled for the day. After all the people who are not working are taken out of the schedule, the remaining agents that are available to handle the incoming contacts will have their breaks and lunches spread out so not everyone is unavailable at once which in turn keeps customers waiting.

Where is my Server?

Imagine for a moment it is the last day of your workweek. You have given everything you have and are worn out and ready for the weekend. To start the weekend out right you decide to go out to dinner with that special someone. You agree upon one of your favorite restaurants and arrive eager to enjoy a wonderful dinner. As you are seated, you find yourself waiting and waiting and waiting. Finally having had enough waiting and being hungry and frustrated you go and get the host/hostess who seated you to find out what the problem is and why you are not being served. After some checking, the host/hostess found out your server decided to go on break outside of their scheduled time! You are asked to go back to your table and wait for your server. Now this might seem a little extreme but remember this next time you think about taking a break or lunch at an unscheduled time. Agents in a contact center are scheduled for their time off the phone when the staffing best allows so that customers may be served as quickly as possible. And while they may not be hungry, they still desire your assistance so make sure to follow your schedule as planned or get approval before making any changes.

How Do I Get My Schedule?

A bid is not something you just see at an auction.

Work schedule bids are used in many contact centers to align the available agents with the forecasted incoming contacts. Bids are when companies distribute a schedule to the workforce and the agents will have a chance to select one of the schedules that best suits their preference. The bid will have various start times and day off combinations available. Work schedules are typically awarded according to some type of ranking such as hire date or performance metrics. The length of a bid can vary and some companies will have weekly bids while others may have one to several bids per year.

When preparing a work schedule bid, skills must be calculated into the mix. A single skill set environment is when an agent is trained in the processing or handling of one specific contact type. A multi-skill set environment is when an agent is trained in the processing or handling of more than one specific contact type. One common application for a multi-skill site is when more than one language is supported. When bidding, agents will usually bid within similar skill groups. An example would be that agents who support Spanish speaking customers may all bid within the same group.

How Many Agents Do We Need?

Staffing requirements are the next step following a forecast that converts the contact volume into how many people you need to hire to service your customers. While contact volume is often mentioned as a driver of required headcount, it is actually something called workload that is most important in determining how many people need to be hired. Workload is simply the contact volume multiplied times the average handle time. So let's say you have 10,000 forecasted contacts to arrive at your contact center and the average handle time is 220 seconds, the total workload would be 2,200,000 units (in seconds). You then take the 2,200,000 seconds and divide this number by the number of work seconds in an hour 3,600 (60 min x 60 sec/min) and you come up with 611 base hours required to handle these contacts. There are still some additional things that must be factored in such as shrinkage and occupancy. Shrinkage makes up those things that take agents away from actually answering calls. Examples of shrinkage are breaks, meetings, vacation, etc. This number can vary greatly but is often between 28 and 32 percent. Occupancy on the other hand is the percentage of time agents are busy while scheduled to take calls. One hundred percent occupancy would mean that an agent is taking one call right after the previous call is complete. This workload for an agent would soon have the agent ready to pull their hair out because there is not breathing room at all. Typically occupancy goals range around the 85 percent plus or minus 5 percent.

So, remembering our 611 required hours from earlier? Divide that number by 1 minus the planned shrinkage number. In this case we will use 30% shrinkage so we divide by 70% (1-30%) and we now have 872 required hours. Factoring in an 85% occupancy goal we now divide the 872 by 85% and our grand total is 1,026 hours required to service the customers. This is an extra 400 hours that must be taken into account when coming up with staffing number.

Forecasting and staffing methods can become very detailed and the purpose here is to simply expose you to the base methodology. Additional factors such as service level and abandon rates should also be calculated in but is beyond the scope of this introduction on staffing requirements. Entire books and courses are dedicated to this very subject of call forecasting and staffing requirements. Hopefully this will give you a sense of the basics of the process as well as an appreciation for the precious call taking time you are scheduled to work.

Day of week distribution

While the best planned contact forecast and
staffing levels will come very close to actual
requirements much of the time, there will also be
times it is off. In order to meet performance
metrics in line, overtime may be offered.
Overtime is also used to cover peaks in the day if
known contact volume spikes exist. Monday
morning is a very common time for spikes or large
volumes of customers in contact centers due to the
number of people returning to work after being off
for the weekend.

When staffing levels are higher than expected,
agents may be offered to go home early without
pay. These are known by many different names
but one common term is "early out".

What is All That Technical Stuff?

Contact Centers have grown tremendously in part by the technology that is now available. Following are some of the basic technologies that are used that you may wish to be familiar with so you can better understand some of the workings behind the scenes.

Automatic Call Distributor (ACD) – A phone system that delivers incoming calls to agents.

Voice Response Unit (VRU) *or Interactive Voice Response Unit* (IVR) – Automated systems that callers hear when calling in. These are the systems that will give you options and then ask you to "press one", etc. The more advanced systems will even use speech recognition and ask you to "press or say one", etc. These systems are used to either automate processes such as checking your savings balance to routing the call to the appropriately trained agent.

Quality Monitoring System – A system that will record the conversation that is taking place between the caller and the agent. The more advanced systems will also record all of the keystrokes that are made as well. These systems are used for coaching purposes and there truly is no better way for you to learn how you sound with a customer than to hear yourself speak.

Inter-queues – These are dedicated phone/data lines that allow a caller to be routed from one call center to another. For instance, if a caller is waiting on hold at one location and an agent is available to handle the call at another location, then the call will be routed via the inter-queue to the other location.

Call routing – The process of how the call will be transferred to the agent. Many scenarios exist for this process but here is an example in its simplest form. The caller may call in and the call routing software may look for an agent trained in only the skill required to handle this call. Should this agent be on another call the software would look for an agent trained in several skill sets. Command centers are often set up in the areas or departments responsible for real time call routing.

Customer Relationship Management (CRM) – With the thousands of customers a company may have, it would be impossible to know them all personally when they call in. One way of knowing about the customer when they call is through the use of CRM software. This software can provide you a profile on your customer that includes information such as previous items purchased, preferences, calling and buying patterns, etc. This allows you to personalize the call to the specific customer resulting in a more personalized customer experience and increased sales. When the customer calls, a lookup of their phone number or account is performed and matched against a database that will automatically display the customer's information on the agent's screen.

Workforce Management Systems – Software that is used to forecast or predict future call volumes and schedule the agents with the incoming call arrival patterns. Analysis is also made much easier via a data feed from the automatic call distributor to the workforce management system. These systems normally have numerous administrative functions as well such as tracking employee information including addresses, skill sets, etc. The most advanced systems may even be used for payroll tracking, real-time adherence monitoring, and reporting.

Predictive Dialer – A system used for outbound calling. These systems will continually dial from a predetermined list of phone numbers. Once a caller answers the phone, the call is immediately routed to an agent who is then able to speak with the person that the predictive dialer was calling. These systems are often used in sales and collections. You may have experienced a time when you answered the phone at home and there was a delay before the person began speaking. If so, you may have been called using a predictive dialer.

Part Four: Your Future

Contact Center Agent 101

Find a Mentor

A mentor is someone you would consider a coach to you. This person is someone who can teach you the ropes of the business.

A good mentor will also introduce you to various people within the organization that can help you get answers to your questions and help you network yourself into greater opportunities. If your company has a formal program on mentoring, make sure to take advantage and get involved with the program. If a formal mentoring program does not exist, take it upon yourself to find someone to model yourself after and ask them if they will work with you. As long as you go in with a specific plan or goal in mind, they should be quite open to working with you to advance your career.

Career Advancement Opportunities

The contact center industry began expanding rapidly in the 1980's and has been exploding in the 2000's. This explosion has created a vast number of career opportunities for people that did not even exist in the contact center industry. Working in a front line production capacity in a contact center may end up being your career aspiration and if that is the case, do not let anyone steer you from this. If you enjoy working with people and truly helping them or feel satisfaction from offering them a product or service they need, then by all means make this your career choice.

The following information is provided for those individuals who would like to become aware of additional opportunities that exist in the contact center industry. Often times, people do not even realize these opportunities are available as professions until they are exposed to them. If there is something here that catches your eye, you are encouraged to find out who is responsible for this task in your organization and see if you can meet with them to learn more.

The first promotion for many agents in a contact center is a lead agent. A lead agent is a person who has a higher level of expertise with their service and/or product and who is also knowledgeable about company procedures that assist other agents. Duties may range from answering questions or explaining how to make a specific computer entry. Another common responsibility of a lead agent may be to handle what is referred to as an escalated call. An escalated call is one where a customer really needs to speak to someone who is able to handle a more challenging situation or that has the authority to provide resolution to the customer's situation.

The next logical step in a contact center person's career path is a supervisor. There are two types of supervisors that exist and each has unique roles and responsibilities. One is an operational supervisor and the other is an administrative supervisor. An operational supervisor has responsibilities with daily front line activities. Tasks including answering agent questions, talking with upset customers, conducting employee reviews, and conducting meetings would be some of the more common activities performed by these front line supervisors. An administrative supervisor handles administrative tasks such as processing work schedule bids, processing vacations, tracking payroll hours, etc. Sometimes reporting is also a responsibility of this position as well.

A manager is the next progression in the career ladder. A manager can either be one of several managers at a site for larger sites or, the manager may be the site manager and be responsible for the entire location. Managers often times have supervisors who report directly to them for which they are responsible for their coaching and mentoring. Managers normally deal with operational issues as well as training and budgeting.

Directors are responsible for the strategic planning of the operation. This person looks to the future and has a vision for where they would like to steer the company from profitability or cost reduction standpoint. Directors are very involved in the budget process as well as telecommunications, and facilities planning. Directors often have managers reporting to them in their span of control.

Your company may also have a Vice President position. If so, this person is even more focused on the vision of the future. In addition, the VP will be very focused on the cost and/or revenue generated by the contact center. This individual may also take a "road show" out and share this vision with others by conducting in person presentations.

Most of the aforementioned positions are in the "operations" area of the contact center. The operations of a contact center are the day-to-day activities. These activities often include the answering calls, making outbound calls, handling customer issues, ensuring real time performance metrics are met, and the interactions between agents, supervisors, and managers.

Some other very important positions also exist in contact centers that are not considered part of the day-to-day operations but part of the administration and planning responsibilities. The first is that of workforce management or workforce planning. Generally, workforce planning consists of those activities that include call forecasting, scheduling, and real time monitoring and routing (routing may also be performed by the telecom area). Each of these responsibilities is critical to the effective operation of the contact center.

Where Are We Headed?

Typically, the higher-level executives will work on strategic planning. Strategic planning is a high level road map of where the company is headed. What are the goals for the next several years? Are any new products or services being rolled out? What will the training program look like over all? What leadership style will be taught? Where will the location of the next contact center be? What type of software applications will be used? These are some of the topics that may be discussed in a strategic planning session.

Global Thinking

When things occur in a contact center it is very easy to fall into the trap of only seeing how it affects the one center you are working in. In reality, if you have other contact centers, what happens in your center can greatly affect these other locations.

Take for instance, an agent who decides to take a break at an unscheduled time. Well, it may have been time for someone at another location to take their break and now the proper numbers of people are no longer available to serve the customer and they have to sit in a call queue to get answered. Multiply this decision several times and the problem only compounds.

What about other things that may occur in a center? If sales are not what they should be and fall below the set goals, then revenues for the company are lessened and this could lead to layoffs, reduced benefits, or reduced marketing, just to name a few.

Your Journey Continues

Contact centers can provide very rewarding careers. The best way to ensure you have a successful experience in the contact center is to first of all make certain you have aligned yourself with a company whose products, services, and culture you like. On occasion, someone will end up working for a company they do not like and make the association all contact centers are bad which will limit your potential greatly. This would make about as much sense as going out to dinner some time and having a bad meal so you decide never to eat out again.

Second, you co-own the relationship and experience with your chosen company and to succeed you must be willing to do your part and then take action to do so. Many people often talk about what they are going to do and then never do it. While it is not required you move up in your organization, you should take a path where you become better each year. Take responsibility for your actions and your future growth.

Continuous Education

If you decide to learn more about your contact center career there are many opportunities for continuing education. The first opportunity to learn more are the people you work with. Learn from other agents, trainers, lead agents, supervisors, managers, directors, and telecommunications team. These people are usually very busy but will often make time for you if you make an appointment.

In addition to the resources you have within your company, many other resources are available to you. Some will cost you a nominal amount of money while others can be much more expensive. The resources are listed and you are encouraged to at least become familiar with them.

Organizations, publications, and resources

- Benchmark Portal
  www.benchmarkportal.com
- Book: Call Center on Fast Forward
  www.icmi.com
- CCNG - Call Center Networking Group
  www.ccng.com
- Contact Center World
  www.contactcenterworld.com
- Gartner Group - www.gartner.com
- Help Desk Institute – www.thinkhdi.com
- ICMI – International Customer Management
  Institute www.icmi.com
- Newton's Telecom Dictionary, Harry
  Newton www.harrynewton.com
- SWPP - Society of Workforce Planning
  Professionals www.swpp.org
- Telephony Magazine
  www.telephonyonline.com
- The Call Center School
  www.thecallcenterschool.com
- The Workforce Management Group
  www.wfmg.com

(Accurate web addresses at time of printing)

Signing Off For the Day

Well, it looks like we have come to the end of our shift and it is time to log out for the day. You are so very important to the success of your company because you are the communication point with your company's customers. Your enjoyment of your career will shine through and make a difference to each and every person you come in contact with.

The purpose of this book was to provide you a basic understanding of call/contact centers. The various types of centers available to work in were discussed, as well as the technologies, and the "why" of why many of the things are done the way they are. You have also been exposed to many of the various careers that are available to you should you decide to expand your horizons into leadership or support functions.

Take this knowledge and embrace your new career. Work hard and give it all you have and truly make a difference to the customers who support your company; after all they help pay for your shelter, car payment, food, clothing, and entertainment. You are important and you do make a difference each and every day. Here is wishing you all the best as you continue on your path to a personally fulfilling contact center career.

About the Author

Steve Stapp has two decades of contact center experience in the multi-site call/contact center environment including operations, staffing, scheduling, forecasting, administration, planning, analysis, budgeting, and reporting. Steve's experience includes leading staff in multiple locations, workforce management and administration of more than 1,500 agents in multi-state call centers, project management, and department/location start-ups. In addition, Steve has more than two decades of customer service experience and more than a decade and a half of leadership experience. Steve's formal education includes a Bachelor of Science Degree in Organizational Communication from Arizona State University. Steve was a member of the Communication Honors program in the College of Public Programs. Steve also holds Associate of Applied Science Degrees in Management and Marketing from Mesa Community College where he graduated Phi Theta Kappa. Most importantly, Steve began on the phones in a contact center and remembers how helpful it was to understand why things are done the way they are and wants to share that information with you!